Plato and Platonism and Related Esoteric Essays

By Helena P. Blavatsky, Thomas Taylor, Alexander Wilder and Fritz Sage Darrow

Copyright © 2019 Lamp of Trismegistus. All rights reserved. No part of this publication may be reproduced or transmitted in any form or by any means, electronic or mechanical, including photocopying, recording, or by any information storage and retrieval system, without permission in writing from Lamp of Trismegistus. Reviewers may quote brief passages.

ISBN: 978-1-63118-432-1

Theosophical Classics

Other Books in this Series and Related Titles

Magical Essays and Instructions by Florence Farr
(978-1-63118-418-5)

Ancient Mysteries and Secret Societies by Manly P. Hall
(978-1-63118-410-9)

The First and Second Gospels of the Infancy of Jesus Christ
by Thomas and James (978-1-63118-415-4)

Lost Atlantis and the Gods of Antiquity & Plato's History of Atlantis
by Carolus Kiesewetterus and Manly P. Hall
(978-1-63118-431-4)

The Human Aura: Astral Colors and Thought Forms by Swami Panchadasi and William Walker Atkinson (978-1-63118-419-2)

The Book of the Watchers by Enoch (978-1-63118-416-1)

The Smoky God or A Voyage to the Inner World
by Willis George Emerson (978-1-63118-423-9)

Rosa Alchemica, The Tables of Law & The Adoration of the Magi
by William Butler Yeats (978-1-63118-421-5)

The Lives of Adam and Eve by Moses (978-1-63118-414-7)

Occult Symbolism of Animals, Insects, Reptiles, Fish and Birds
by Manly P. Hall (978-1-63118-420-8)

The Feminine Occult by various authors (978-1-63118-711-7)

Essays on the Esoteric Tradition of Karma by Helena P. Blavatsky, William Q. Judge & Annie Besant (978-1-63118-426-0)

Audio Versions are also Available on Audible and iTunes

Table of Contents

Introduction...7

The Teachings of Plato
by Alexander Wilder...9

-oOo-

Plato and Platonism
by Helena P. Blavatsky...19

-oOo-

The Platonic Philosopher's Creed
by Thomas Taylor...35

-oOo-

Plato's Conception of the Function of True Art
by Fritz Sage Darrow...45

Introduction

The Theosophical movement of the late nineteenth century provided the world with an extensive canon of literature related to a wide variety of esoteric subjects. Theosophical publications were proliferous, producing thousands of articles on such subjects as mysticism, astral projection, Rosicrucianism, Greek philosophy, alchemy, Qabalah, Hinduism and Buddhism, Hermeticism and so on. Throughout this material, the unifying factor was always altruism and the concept of a Universal Brotherhood. Readers eagerly consumed these new ideas; however, with the passage of time, challenging world events, new pass-times and the ever-changing interests of our society, many of these works have fallen to the wayside and become nearly forgotten.

Lamp of Trismegistus is doing its part to help preserve humanity's spiritual history, by making some of these classics available to those students who are seeking to unearth the knowledge of these ancient colossi. As such, Lamp of Trismegistus offers its readers highlights of esoteric study, culled from a variety of authors and viewpoints, with the hope bringing education back into the forefront of our theosophical and spiritual lives. So, be sure to check out other titles in our *Theosophical Classics* collection as well as our *Foundations of Freemasonry Series, Esoteric Classics, Occult Fiction* and our *Christian Apocrypha Series*, and don't be afraid to let a little altruism into your own heart or even into your inner sanctum. You can also download the audio versions of most of these titles from iTunes or Audible for learning on the go.

The Teachings of Plato
By Alexander Widler

"'Eagle! why soarest thou above that tomb?
To what sublime and starry-paven home
Floatest thou?'
'I am the image of great Plato's spirit
Ascending heaven; Athens doth inherit
His corpse below.'"

"Out of Plato" says Ralph Waldo Emerson "come all things that are still written and debated among men of thought." All else seems ephemeral, perishing with the day. The science and mechanic arts of the present time, which are prosecuted with so much assiduity, are superficial and short-lived. When Doctor James Simpson succeeded his distinguished uncle at the University of Edinburgh, he directed the librarian to remove the text-books which were more than ten years old, as obsolete. The skilled inventions and processes in mechanism have hardly a longer duration. Those which were exhibited at the first World's Fair in 1851 are now generally gone out of use, and those displayed at the Centennial Exhibition at Philadelphia in 1876 are fast giving place to newer ones that serve the purposes better. All the science which is comprised within the purview of the senses, is in like manner, unstable and subject to transmutation. What appears today to be fundamental fact is very certain to be found, tomorrow, to be dependent upon something beyond. It is like the rustic's hypothesis that the earth stands upon a rock, and that upon another rock, and so on; there being rocks all the way down. But Philosophy, penetrating to the profounder truth and including the Over-Knowledge in its field, never grows old, never becomes out of date, but abides through the ages in perennial freshness.

The style and even the tenor of the *Dialogues* have been criticized, either from misapprehension of their purport or from a desire to disparage Plato himself. There is a vanity for being regarded as original, or as first to open the way into a new field of thought and investigation, which is sometimes as deep-seated as a cancer and about as difficult to eradicate. From this, however, Plato was entirely free. His personality is everywhere; veiled by his philosophy.

At the time when Plato flourished, the Grecian world had undergone great revolutions. The former times had passed away. Herakles and Theseus, the heroes of the Myths, were said to have vanquished the manslaying monsters of the worship of Hippa and Poseidon, or in other words supplanting the Pelasgian period by the Hellenic and Ionian. The arcane rites of Demeter had been softened and made to represent a drama of soul-history. The Tragedians had also modified and popularized the worship of Dionysus at the Theatre-Temple of Athens. Philosophy, first appearing in Ionia had come forth into bolder view, and planted itself upon the firm foundation of psychologic truth. Plato succeeded to all, to the Synthetists of the Mysteries, the Dramatists of the Stage, to Socrates and those who had been philosophers before him.

Great as he was, he was the outcome of the best thought of his time. In a certain sense there has been no new religion. Every world-faith has come from older ones as the result of new inspiration, and Philosophy has its source in religious veneration. Plato himself recognized the archaic Wisdom-Religion as "the most unalloyed form of worship, to the

Philosophy of which, in primitive ages, Zoroaster made many additions drawn from the Mysteries of the Chaldeans." When the Persian influence extended into Asia Minor, there sprung up philosophers in Ionia and Greece. The further progress of the religion of Mazda was arrested at Salamis, but the evangel of the Pure Thought, Pure Word, and Pure Deed was destined to permeate the Western World during the succeeding ages. Plato gave voice to it, and we find the marrow of the Oriental Wisdom in his dialectic. He seems to have joined the occult lore of the East, the conceptions of other teachers, and the under-meaning of the arcane rites, the physical and metaphysical learning of India and Asia, and wrought the whole into forms adapted to European comprehension.

His leading discourses, those which are most certainly genuine, are characterized by the inductive method. He displays a multitude of particulars for the purpose of inferring a general truth. He does not endeavor so much to implant his own conviction as to enable the hearer and reader to attain one intelligently, for themselves. He is in quest of principles, and leading the argument to that goal. Some of the *Dialogues* are described as after the manner of the Bacchic dithyrambic, spoken or chanted at the Theatre; others are transcripts of Philosophic conversations. Plato was not so much teaching as showing others how to learn.

His aim was to set forth the nature of man and the end of his being. The great questions of who, whence and whither, comprise what he endeavored to illustrate. Instead of dogmatic affirmation, the arbitrary *ipse dixit* of Pythagoras and his oath of secrecy, we have a friend, one like ourselves, familiarly and patiently leading us on to investigation as though we were doing it of our own accord. Arrogance and pedantic assumption were out of place in the Academy.

The whole Platonic teaching is based upon the concept of Absolute Goodness. Plato was vividly conscious of the immense profundity of the subject. "To discover the Creator and Father of this universe, as well as his operation, is indeed difficult; and when discovered it is impossible to reveal him." In him Truth, Justice and the Beautiful are eternally one. Hence the idea of the Good is the highest branch of study.

There is a criterion by which to know the truth, and Plato sought it out. The perceptions of sense fail utterly to furnish it. The law of right for example, is not the law of the strongest, but what is always expedient for the strongest. The criterion is therefore no less than the conceptions innate in every human soul. These relate to that which is true, because it is ever-abiding. What is true is always right — right and therefore supreme: eternal and therefore always good. In its inmost essence it is Being itself; in its form by which we are able to contemplate it, it is justice and virtue in the concepts of essence, power and energy.

These concepts are in every human soul and determine all forms of our thought. We encounter them in our most common experiences and recognize them as universal principles, infinite and absolute. However latent and dormant they may seem, they are ready to be aroused, and they enable us to distinguish spontaneously the wrong from the right. They are memories, we are assured, that belong to our inmost being, and to the eternal world. They accompanied the soul into this region of time, of ever-becoming and of sense. The soul, therefore, or rather its inmost spirit or intellect, is of and from eternity. It is not so much an inhabitant of the world of nature as a sojourner from the eternal region. Its trend and ulterior destination are accordingly toward the beginning from which it originally set out.

The Vision of Eros in the tenth book of the *Republic* suggests the archaic conception generally entertained that human beings dying from the earth are presently born into new forms of existence, till the three Weird Sisters shall have finished their task and the circle of Necessity is completed. The events of each succeeding term of life take a direction from what has occurred before. Much may be imputed to heredity, but not all. This is implied in the question of the disciples to Jesus: "Which sinned, this person or his parents, that he should be born blind." We all are conscious of some occurrence or experience that seems to pertain to a former term of life. It appears to us as if we had witnessed scenes before, which must be some recollection, except it be a remembrance inherited from ancestors, or some spiritual essence has transferred it as from a *camera obscura* into our consciousness. We may account it certain, at any rate, that we are inhabitants of eternity, and of that eternity Time is as a colonial possession and distinct allotment.

Everything pertaining to this world of time and sense, is constantly changing, and whatever it discloses to us is illusive. The laws and reasons of things must be found out elsewhere. We must search in the world which is beyond appearances, beyond sensation and its illusions. There are in all minds certain qualities or principles which underlie our faculty of knowing. These principles are older than experience, for they govern it; and while they combine more or less with our observations, they are superior and universal, and they are apprehended by us as infinite and absolute. They are our memories of the life of the eternal world, and it is the province of the philosophic discipline to call them into activity as the ideals of goodness and truth and beauty, and thus awaken the soul to the cognizing of God.

This doctrine of ideas or idealities lies at the foundation of the Platonic teachings. It assumes first of all, the presence and operation of the Supreme Intelligence, an essence which transcends and contains the principles of goodness, truth, and order. Every form or ideal, every relation and every principle of right must be ever present to the Divine Thought. Creation in all its details is necessarily the image and manifestation of these ideas. "That which imparts truth to knowable things," says Plato, "that which gives to the knower the power of knowing the truth, is the Idea of the Good, and you are to conceive of this as the Source of knowledge and truth."

A cognition of the phenomena of the universe may not be considered as a real knowing. We must perceive that which is stable and unchanging, — *that which really is*. It is not enough to be able to regard what is beautiful and contemplate right conduct. The philosopher, the lover of wisdom, looks beyond these to the Actual Beauty, — to righteousness itself. This is the *episteme* of Plato, the superior, transcendent knowing. This knowledge is actual participating in the eternal principles themselves — the possessing of them as elements of our own being.

Upon this, Plato bases the doctrine of our immortality. These principles, the ideals of truth, beauty and goodness are eternal, and those who possess them are ever-living. The learning of them is simply the bringing of them into conscious remembrance.

In regard to Evil, Plato did not consider it as inherent in human nature. "Nobody is willingly evil," he declares; "but when any one does evil it is only as the imagined means to some good end. But in the nature of things, there must always be a something contrary to good. It cannot have its seat with the gods, being utterly opposed to them, and so of necessity hovers round this finite mortal nature, and this region of time and ever-changing. Wherefore," he declares, "we ought to fly hence." He does not mean that we ought to hasten to die, for he taught that nobody could escape from evil or eliminate it from himself by dying. This flight is effected by resembling God as much as is possible; "and this resemblance consists in becoming just and holy through wisdom." There is no divine anger or favor to be propitiated; nothing else than a becoming like the One, absolutely good.

When Euthyphro explained that whatever is pleasing to the gods is holy, and that that which is hateful to them is impious, Socrates appealed to the statements of the Poets, that there were angry differences between the gods, so that the things and persons that were acceptable to some of them were hateful to the others. Everything holy and sacred must also be just. Thus he suggested a criterion to determine the matter, to which every god in the Pantheon must be subject. They were subordinate beings, and as is elsewhere taught, are younger than the Demiurges.

No survey of the teachings of the Academy, though only intended to be partial, will be satisfactory which omits a mention of the Platonic Love. Yet it is essential to regard the subject philosophically. For various reasons our philosopher speaks much in metaphor, and they who construe his language in literal senses will often err. His *Banquet* is a symposium of thought, and in no proper sense a drinking bout. He is always moral, and when in his discourse he begins familiarly with things as they existed around him, it was with a direct purpose to lead up to what they are when absolutely right. Love, therefore, which is recognized as a complacency and attraction between human beings, he declares to be unprolific of higher intellect. It is his aim to exalt it to an aspiration for the higher and better. The mania or inspiration of Love is the greatest of Heaven's blessings, he declares, and it is given for the sake of producing the greatest blessedness. "What is Love?" asked Socrates of the God-honored Mantineke. "He is a great daemon," she replies, "and, like all daemons, is intermediate between Divinity and mortal. He interprets between gods and men, conveying to the gods the prayers and sacrifices of men, and to men the commands and replies of the gods. He is the mediator who spans the chasm that divides them; in him all is bound together and through him the arts of the prophet and priest, their sacrifices and initiations and charms, and all prophecy and incantation find their way. For God mingles not with men, but through Love all the intercourse and speech of God with men, whether awake or asleep, is carried on. The wisdom which understands this is spiritual; all other wisdom, such as that of arts or handicrafts, is mean and vulgar. Now these spiritual essences or intermediaries are many and diverse, and one of them is Love."

It is manifest then, that Plato emulates no mere physical attraction, no passionless friendship, but an ardent, amorous quest of the Soul for the Good and the True. It surpasses the former as the sky exceeds the earth. Plato describes it in glowing terms: "We, having been initiated and admitted to the beatific vision, journeyed with the chorus of heaven; beholding ravishing beauties ineffable and possessing transcendent knowledge; for we were freed from the contamination of that earth to which we are bound here, as an oyster to his shell."

In short, goodness was the foundation of his ethics, and a divine intuition the core of all his doctrines.

When, however, we seek after detail and formula for a

religious or philosophic system, Plato fails us. Herein each must minister to himself. The Academy comprised method rather than system; how to know the truth, what fields to explore, what tortuous paths and pitfalls to shun. Everyone is left free in heart and mind to deduce his own conclusions. It is the Truth, and not Plato or any other teacher, that makes us free. And we are free only in so far as we perceive the Supernal Beauty and apprehend the Good.

Plato and Platonism

By Helena P. Blavatsky

The whole question of phenomena rests on the correct comprehension of old philosophies. Whither, then, should we turn, in our perplexity, but to the ancient sages, since, on the pretext of superstition, we are refused an explanation by the modern? Let us ask them what they know of genuine science and religion; not in the matter of mere details, but in all the broad conception of these twin truths -- so strong in their unity, so weak when divided. Besides, we may find our profit in comparing this boasted modern science with ancient ignorance; this improved modern theology with the "secret doctrines" of the ancient universal religion. Perhaps we may thus discover a neutral ground whence we can reach and profit by both.

It is the Platonic philosophy, the most elaborate compend of the abstruse systems of old India that can alone afford us this middle ground. Although twenty- two and a quarter centuries have elapsed since the death of Plato, the great minds of the world are still occupied with his writings. He was, in the fullest sense of the word, the world's interpreter. And the greatest philosopher of the pre-Christian era mirrored faithfully in his works the spiritualism of the Vedic philosophers who lived thousands of years before himself, and its metaphysical expression. Vyasa, Djeminy, Kapila, Vrihaspati, Sumati, and so many others, will be found to have transmitted their indelible imprint through the intervening centuries upon Plato and his school. Thus is warranted the inference that to Plato and the ancient Hindu sages was alike revealed the same wisdom. So surviving the shock of time, what can this wisdom be but divine and eternal?

Plato taught justice as subsisting in the soul of its possessor and his greatest good. "Men, in proportion to their intellect, have admitted his transcendent claims." Yet his commentators, almost with one consent, shrink from every passage which implies that his metaphysics are based on a solid foundation, and not on ideal conceptions.

But Plato could not accept a philosophy destitute of spiritual aspirations; the two were at one with him. For the old Grecian sage there was a single object of attainment: REAL KNOWLEDGE. He considered those only to be genuine philosophers, or students of truth, who possess the knowledge of the really- existing, in opposition to the mere seeing; of the *always-existing,* in opposition to the transitory; and of that which exists *permanently,* in opposition to that which waxes, wanes, and is developed and destroyed alternately. "Beyond all finite existences and secondary causes, all laws, ideas, and principles, there is an INTELLIGENCE or MIND, the first principle of all principles, the Supreme Idea on which all other ideas are grounded; the Monarch and

Lawgiver of the universe; the ultimate substance from which all things derive their being and essence, the first and efficient Cause of all the order, and harmony, and beauty, and excellency, and goodness, which pervades the universe -- who is called, by way of preeminence and excellence, the Supreme Good, the God, 'the God over all.' " He is not the truth nor the intelligence, but "the father of it." Though this eternal essence of things may not be perceptible by our physical senses, it may be apprehended by the mind of those who are not willfully obtuse. "To you," said Jesus to his elect disciples, "it is given to know the mysteries of the Kingdom of God, but to them [the polloi] it is not given; . . . therefore speak I to them in parables; because they seeing, see not, and hearing, they hear not, neither do they understand." (Gospel according to Matthew, chapter xiii., verses 11-13)

The philosophy of Plato, we are assured by Porphyry, of the Neoplatonic School was taught and illustrated in the MYSTERIES. Many have questioned and even denied this; and Lobeck, in his *Aglaophomus,* has gone to the extreme of representing the sacred orgies as little more than an empty show to captivate the imagination. As though Athens and Greece would for twenty centuries and more have repaired every fifth year to Eleusis to witness a solemn religious farce! Augustine, the papa- bishop of Hippo, has resolved such assertions. He declares that the doctrines of the Alexandrian Platonists were the original esoteric doctrines of the first followers of Plato, and describes Plotinus as a Plato resuscitated. He also explains the motives of the great philosopher for veiling the interior sense of what he taught.

"The accusations of atheism, the introducing of foreign deities, and corrupting of the Athenian youth, which were made against Socrates, afforded ample justification for Plato to conceal the arcane preaching of his doctrines. Doubtless the peculiar diction or 'jargon' of the alchemists was employed for a like purpose. The dungeon, the rack, and the fagot were employed without scruple by Christians of every shade, the Roman Catholics especially, against all who taught even natural science contrary to the theories entertained by the Church. Pope Gregory the Great even inhibited the grammatical use of Latin as heathenish. The offense of Socrates consisted in unfolding to his disciples the arcane doctrine concerning the gods, which was taught in the Mysteries and was a capital crime. He also was charged by Aristophanes with introducing the new god Dinos into the republic as the demiurgos or artificer, and the lord of the solar universe. The Heliocentric system was also a doctrine of the Mysteries; and hence, when Aristarchus the

Pythagorean taught it openly, Cleanthes declared that the Greeks ought to have called him to account and condemned him for blasphemy against the gods," -- ("Plutarch").

But Socrates had never been initiated, and hence divulged nothing which had ever been imparted to him. As to the *myths,* Plato declares in the *Gorgias* and the *Phaedon* that they were the vehicles of great truths well worth the seeking. But commentators are so little *en rapport* with the great philosopher as to be compelled to acknowledge that they are ignorant where "the doctrinal ends, and the mythical begins." Plato put to flight the popular superstition concerning magic and daemons, and developed the exaggerated notions of the time into rational theories and metaphysical conceptions. Perhaps these would not quite stand the inductive method of reasoning established by Aristotle; nevertheless they are satisfactory in the highest degree to those who apprehend the existence of that higher faculty of insight or intuition, as affording a criterion for ascertaining truth.

Basing all his doctrines upon the presence of the Supreme Mind, Plato taught that the *nous,* spirit, or rational soul of man, being "generated by the Divine Father," possessed a nature kindred, or even homogeneous, with the Divinity, and was capable of beholding the eternal realities. This faculty of contemplating reality in a direct and immediate manner belongs to God alone; the aspiration for this knowledge constitutes what is really meant by *philosophy* -- the love of wisdom. The love of truth is inherently the love of good; and so predominating over every desire of the soul, purifying it and assimilating it to the divine, thus governing every act of the individual, it raises man to a participation and communion with Divinity, and restores him to the likeness of God. "This flight," says Plato in the *Theaetetus,* "consists in becoming like God, and this assimilation is the becoming just and holy with wisdom."

The basis of this assimilation is always asserted to be the preexistence of the spirit or *nous*. In the allegory of the chariot and winged steeds, given in the *Phaedrus,* he represents the psychical nature as composite and two-fold; the *thumos,* or *epithumetic* part, formed from the substances of the world of phenomena; and the *thumoeides,* the essence of which is linked to the eternal world. The present earth-life is a fall and punishment. The soul dwells in "the grave which we call *the body,*" and in its incorporate state, and previous to the discipline of education, the noetic or spiritual element is "asleep." Life is thus a dream, rather than a reality. Like the captives in the subterranean cave, described in *The Republic,* the back is turned to the light, we perceive only the shadows of objects, and think them the actual realities. Is not this the idea of *Maya,* or the illusion of the senses in physical life, which is so marked a feature in Buddhistical philosophy? But these shadows, if we have not given ourselves up absolutely to the sensuous nature, arouse in us the reminiscence of that higher world that we once inhabited. "The interior spirit has some dim and shadowy recollection of its ante-natal state of bliss, and some instinctive and proleptic yearnings for its return." It is the province of the discipline of philosophy to disenthrall it from the bondage of sense, and raise it into the empyrean of pure thought, to the vision of eternal truth, goodness, and beauty. "The soul," says Plato, in the *Theaetetus,* "cannot come into the form of a man if it has never seen the truth. This is a recollection of those things which our soul formerly saw when journeying with Deity, despising the things which we now say *are,* and looking up to that which REALLY is. Wherefore the *nous,* or spirit, of the philosopher (or student of the higher truth) alone is furnished with wings; because he, to the best of his ability, keeps these things in mind, of which the contemplation renders even Deity itself divine. By making the right use of these things remembered from the former life, by constantly perfecting himself in the perfect mysteries, a man becomes truly perfect -- an initiate into the diviner wisdom."

Hence we may understand why the sublimer scenes in the Mysteries were always in the night. The life of the interior spirit is the death of the external nature; and the night of the physical world denotes the day of the spiritual. Dionysus, the night-sun, is, therefore, worshipped rather than Helios, orb of day. In the Mysteries were symbolized the preexistent condition of the spirit and soul, and the lapse of the latter into earth-life and Hades, the miseries of that life, the purification of the soul, and its restoration to divine bliss, or reunion with spirit. Theon, of Smyrna, aptly compares the philosophical discipline to the mystic rites: "Philosophy," says he, "may be called the initiation into the true arcana, and the instruction in the genuine Mysteries. There are five parts of this initiation: I., the previous purification; II., the admission to participation in the arcane rites; III., the epoptic revelation; IV., the investiture or enthroning; V. -- the fifth, which is produced from all these, is friendship and interior communion with God, and the enjoyment of that felicity which arises from intimate converse with divine beings. . . . Plato denominates the *epopteia,* or personal view, the perfect contemplation of things which are apprehended intuitively, absolute truths and ideas. He also considers the binding of the head and crowning as analogous to the authority which any one receives from his instructors, of leading others into the same contemplation. The fifth gradation is the most perfect felicity arising from hence, and, according to Plato, an assimilation to divinity as far as is possible to human beings."

Such is Platonism. "Out of Plato," says Ralph Waldo Emerson, "come all things that are still written and debated among men of thought." He absorbed the learning of his times -- of Greece from Phiolaus to Socrates; then of Pythagoras in

Italy; then what he could procure from Egypt and the East. He was so broad that all philosophy, European and Asiatic, was in his doctrines; and to culture and contemplation he added the nature and qualities of the poet.

The followers of Plato generally adhered strictly to his psychological theories. Several, however, like Xenocrates, ventured into bolder speculations. Speusippus, the nephew and successor of the great philosopher, was the author of the *Numerical Analysis,* a treatise on the Pythagorean numbers. Some of his speculations are not found in the written *Dialogues;* but as he was a listener to the unwritten lectures of Plato, the judgment of Enfield is doubtless correct, that he did not differ from his master. He was evidently, though not named, the antagonist whom Aristotle criticized, when professing to cite the argument of Plato against the doctrine of Pythagoras, that all things were in themselves numbers, or rather, inseparable from the idea of numbers. He especially endeavored to show that the Platonic doctrine of ideas differed essentially from the Pythagorean, in that it presupposed numbers and magnitudes to exist apart from things. He also asserted that Plato taught that there could be no *real* knowledge, if the object of that knowledge was not carried beyond or above the sensible.

But Aristotle was no trustworthy witness. He misrepresented Plato, and he almost caricatured the doctrines of Pythagoras. There is a canon of interpretation, which should guide us in our examinations of every philosophical opinion: "The human mind has, under the necessary operation of its own laws, been compelled to entertain the same fundamental ideas, and the human heart to cherish the same feelings in all ages." It is certain that Pythagoras awakened the deepest intellectual sympathy of his age, and that his doctrines exerted a powerful influence upon the mind of Plato. His cardinal idea was that there existed a permanent principle of unity beneath the forms, changes, and other phenomena of the universe. Aristotle asserted that he taught that "numbers are the first principles of all entities." Ritter has expressed the opinion that the formula of Pythagoras should be taken symbolically, which is doubtless correct. Aristotle goes on to associate these *numbers* with the "forms" and "ideas" of Plato. He even declares that Plato said: "forms are numbers," and that "ideas are substantial existences -- real beings." Yet Plato did not so teach. He declared that the final cause was the Supreme Goodness -- *to Agathon*. "Ideas are objects of pure conception for the human reason, and they are attributes of the Divine Reason." Nor did he ever say that "forms are numbers." What he did say may be found in the *Timaeus:* "God formed things as they first arose according to forms and numbers."

It is recognized by modern science that all the higher laws of nature assume the form of quantitative statement. This is perhaps a fuller elaboration or more explicit affirmation of the Pythagorean doctrine. Numbers were regarded as the best representations of the laws of harmony which pervade the cosmos. We know too that in chemistry the doctrine of atoms and the laws of combination are actually and, as it were, arbitrarily defined by numbers. As Mr. W. Archer Butler has expressed it: "The world is, then, through all its departments, a living arithmetic in its development, a realized geometry in its repose."

The key to the Pythagorean dogmas is the general formula of unity in multiplicity, the one evolving the many and pervading the many. This is the ancient doctrine of emanation in few words. Even the apostle Paul accepted it as true. "Out of him and through him and in him all things are." This, as we can see by the following quotation, is purely Hindu and Brahmanical:

> "When the dissolution -- Pralaya -- had arrived at its term, the great Being -- Para-Atma or Para- Purusha --

the Lord existing through himself, out of whom and through whom all things were, and are and will be . . . resolved to emanate from his own substance the various creatures"

The mystic Decad $1 + 2 + 3 + 4 = 10$ is a way of expressing this idea. The One is God, the Two, matter; the Three, combining Monad and Duad, and partaking of the nature of both, is the phenomenal world; the Tetrad, or form of perfection, expresses the emptiness of all; and the Decad, or sum of all, involves the entire cosmos. The universe is the combination of a thousand elements, and yet the expression of a single spirit -- a chaos to the sense, a cosmos to the reason.

The whole of this combination of the progression of numbers in the idea of creation is Hindu. The Being existing through himself, Swayambhu or Swayambhuva, as he is called by some, is one. He emanates from himself the *creative faculty*, Brahma or Purusha (the divine male), and the one becomes *Two*; out of this Duad, union of the purely intellectual principle with the principle of matter, evolves a third, which is Viradj, the phenomenal world. It is out of this invisible and incomprehensible trinity, the Brahmanic Trimurty, that evolves the second triad which represents the three faculties -- the creative, the conservative, and the transforming. These are typified by Brahma, Vishnu, and Siva, but are again and ever blended into one. *Unity*, Brahma, or as the *Vedas* called him, Tridandi, is the god triply manifested, which gave rise to the symbolical *Aum* or the abbreviated Trimurty. It is but under this trinity, ever active and tangible to all our senses, that the invisible and unknown Monas can manifest itself to the world of mortals. When he becomes *Sarira,* or he who puts on a visible form, he typifies all the principles of matter, all the germs of life, he is Purusha, the god of the three visages, or triple power, the essence of the Vedic triad. "Let the Brahmas know the sacred Syllable (Aum), the three words of the Savitri, and read the *Vedas* daily."

He who has studied Pythagoras and his speculations on the Monad, which, after having emanated the Duad retires into silence and darkness, and thus creates the Triad can realize whence came the philosophy of the great Samian Sage, and after him that of Socrates and Plato.

Speusippus seems to have taught that the psychical or thumetic soul was immortal as well as the spirit or rational soul, and further on we will show his reasons. He also -- like Philolaus and Aristotle, in his disquisitions upon the soul -- makes of aether an element; so that there were five principal elements to correspond with the five regular figures in Geometry. This became also a doctrine of the Alexandrian school. Indeed, there was much in the doctrines of the *Philaletheans* which did not appear in the works of the older Platonists, but was doubtless taught in substance by the philosopher himself, but with his usual reticence was not committed to writing as being too arcane for promiscuous publication. Speusippus and Xenocrates after him, held, like their great master, that the *anima mundi,* or world-soul, was not the Deity, but a manifestation. Those philosophers never conceived of the One as an *animate nature.* The original One did not *exist,* as we understand the term. Not till he had united with the many -- emanated existence (the monad and duad) was a being produced. The *timion,* honored -- the something manifested, dwells in the center as in the circumference, but it is only the reflection of the Deity -- the World-Soul. In this doctrine we find the spirit of esoteric Buddhism.

A man's idea of God, is that image of blinding light that he sees reflected in the concave mirror of his own soul, and yet this is not, in very truth, God, but only His reflection. His glory is there, but, it is the light of his own Spirit that the man sees, and it is all he can bear to look upon. *The clearer the mirror, the brighter will be the divine image.* But the external world cannot be witnessed in it at the same moment. In the ecstatic Yogi, in the illuminated Seer, the spirit will shine like the noonday sun; in the debased victim of earthly attraction, the radiance has disappeared, for the mirror is obscured with the stains of matter. Such men deny their God, and would willingly deprive humanity of soul at one blow.

Though some have considered Speusippus as inferior to Aristotle, the world is nevertheless indebted to him for defining and expounding many things that Plato had left obscure in his doctrine of the Sensible and Ideal. His maxim was "The Immaterial is known by means of scientific thought, the Material by scientific perception."

Xenocrates expounded many of the unwritten theories and teachings of his master. He too held the Pythagorean doctrine, and his system of numerals and mathematics in the highest estimation. Recognizing but three degrees of knowledge -- *Thought, Perception,* and *Envisagement* (or knowledge by *Intuition*), he made the former busy itself with all that which is *beyond* the heavens: Perception with things in the heavens; Intuition with the heavens themselves.

We find again these theories, and nearly in the same language in the *Manava-Dharma-Sastra*, when speaking -- of the creation of man: "He (the Supreme) drew from his own essence the immortal breath which *perisheth not in the being,* and to this soul of the being he gave the Ahancara (conscience of the *ego*) sovereign guide. Then he gave to that soul of the being (man) the intellect formed of *the three qualities,* and the five organs of the outward perception."

These three qualities are Intelligence, Conscience, and Will; answering to the Thought, Perception, and Envisagement of Xenocrates. The relation of numbers to Ideas was developed by him further than by Speusippus, and he surpassed Plato in his definition of the doctrine of Invisible Magnitudes. Reducing them to their ideal primary elements, he demonstrated that every figure and form originated out of the smallest indivisible line. That Xenocrates held the same theories as Plato in relation to the human soul is evident, though Aristotle contradicts this, like every other teaching of this philosopher. This is conclusive evidence that many of Plato's doctrines were delivered orally, even were it shown that Xenocrates and not Plato was the first to originate the theory of indivisible magnitudes. He derives the Soul from the first Duad, and calls it a self-moved number.

Theophrastus remarks that he entered and eliminated this Soul-theory more than any other Platonist. He built upon it the cosmological doctrine, and proved the necessary existence in every part of the universal space of a successive and progressive series of animated and thinking though spiritual beings. The Human Soul with him is a compound of the most spiritual properties of the Monad and the Duad, possessing the highest principles of both. If, like Plato and Prodicus, he refers to the Elements as to Divine Powers, and calls them gods, neither himself nor others connected any anthropomorphic idea with the appellation. Krische remarks that he called them gods only that these elementary powers should not be confounded with the daemons of the nether world (the Elementary Spirits). As the Soul of the World permeates the whole Cosmos, even beasts must have in them something divine. This, also, is the doctrine of Buddhists and the Hermetists, and Manu endows with a living soul even the plants and the tiniest blade of grass.

The daemons, according to this theory, are intermediate beings between the divine perfection and human sinfulness, and Plutarch divides them into classes, each subdivided in many others. But he states expressly that the individual or personal soul is the leading guardian daemon of every man, and that no daemon has more power over us than our own. Thus the *Daimonion* of Socrates is the god or Divine Entity which inspired him all his life. It depends on man either to open or close his perceptions to the Divine voice. Like Speusippus he ascribed immortality to the *psyche*, psychical body, or irrational soul. But some Hermetic philosophers have taught that the soul has a separate continued existence only so long as in its passage through the spheres any material or earthly particles remain incorporated in it; and that when absolutely purified, the latter are *annihilated,* and the quintessence of the soul alone becomes blended with its *divine* spirit (the *Rational),* and the two are thenceforth one.

Zeller states that Xenocrates forbade the eating of animal food, not because he saw in beasts something akin to man, as he ascribed to them a dim consciousness of God, but, "for the opposite reason, lest the irrationality of animal souls might thereby obtain a certain influence over us." But we believe that it was rather because, like Pythagoras, he had had the Hindu sages for his masters and models. Cicero depicted Xenocrates utterly despising everything except the highest virtue; and describes the stainlessness and severe austerity of his character. "To free ourselves from the subjection of sensuous existence, to conquer the Titanic elements in our terrestrial nature through the Divine one, is our problem." Zeller makes him say: "Purity, even in the secret longings of our heart, is the greatest duty, and only philosophy and the initiation into the Mysteries help toward the attainment of this object." Crantor, another philosopher associated with the earliest days of Plato's Academy, conceived the human soul as formed out of the primary substance of all things, the Monad or One, and the Duad or the Two. Plutarch speaks at length of this philosopher, who like his master believed in souls being distributed in earthly bodies as an exile and punishment.

Herakleides, though some critics do not believe him to have strictly adhered to Plato's primal philosophy taught the same ethics. Zeller presents him to us imparting, like Hicetas and Ecphantus, the Pythagorean doctrine of the diurnal rotation of the earth and the immobility of the fixed stars, but adds that he was ignorant of the annual revolution of the earth around the sun, and of the heliocentric system. But we have good evidence that the latter system was taught in the Mysteries, and that Socrates died for *atheism, i.e.,* for divulging this sacred knowledge. Herakleides adopted fully the Pythagorean and Platonic views of the human soul, its faculties and its capabilities. He describes it as a luminous, highly ethereal essence. He affirms that souls inhabit the milky way before descending "into generation" or sublunary existence. His daemons or spirits are airy and vaporous bodies.

In the *Epinomis* is fully stated the doctrine of the Pythagorean numbers in relation to created things. As a true Platonist, its author maintains that wisdom can only be attained by a thorough inquiry into the occult nature of the creation; it alone assures us an existence of bliss after death. The immortality of the soul is greatly speculated upon in this treatise; but its author adds that we can attain to this knowledge only through a complete comprehension of the numbers; for the man, unable to distinguish the straight line from a curved one will never have wisdom enough to secure a mathematical demonstration of the *invisible, i.e.,* we must assure ourselves of the objective existence of our soul (astral body) before we learn that we are in possession of a divine and immortal spirit. Iamblichus says the same thing; adding, moreover, that it is a secret belonging to the highest initiation. The Divine Power, he says, always felt indignant with those "who rendered manifest the composition of the *icostagonus,"* viz., who delivered the method of inscribing in a sphere the dodecahedron (one of the five solid figures in Geometry.).

The idea that "numbers" possessing the greatest virtue, produce always what is good and never what is evil, refers to justice, equanimity of temper, and everything that is harmonious. When the author speaks of every star as an individual soul, he only means what the Hindu initiates and the Hermetists taught before and after him, viz.: that every star is an independent planet, which, like our earth, has a soul of its own, every atom of matter being impregnated with the divine influx of the soul of the world. It breathes and lives; it feels and suffers as well as enjoys life in its way. What naturalist is prepared to dispute it on good evidence? Therefore, we must consider the celestial bodies as the images of gods; as partaking of the divine powers in their substance; and though they are not immortal in their soul-entity, their agency in the economy of the universe is entitled to divine honors, such as we pay to minor gods. The idea is plain, and one must be malevolent indeed to misrepresent it. If the author of *Epinomis* places these fiery gods higher than the animals, plants, and even mankind, all of which, as earthly creatures, are assigned by him a lower place, who can prove him wholly wrong? One must need go deep indeed into the profundity of the abstract metaphysics of the old philosophies, who would understand that their various embodiments of their conceptions are, after all, based upon an identical apprehension of the nature of the First Cause, its attributes and method.

Again when the author of *Epinomis* locates between these highest and lowest gods (embodied souls) three classes of daemons, and peoples the universe with invisible beings, he is more rational than our modern scientists, who make between the two extremes one vast hiatus of being, the playground of blind forces. Of these three classes the first two are invisible; their bodies are pure ether and fire (*planetary spirits*); the daemons of the third class are clothed with vapory bodies; they are usually invisible, but sometimes making themselves concrete become visible for a few seconds. These are the earthly spirits, or our astral souls.

It is these doctrines, which, studied analogically, and on the principle of correspondence, led the ancient, and may now lead the modern Philaletheian step by step toward the solution of the greatest mysteries. On the brink of the dark chasm separating the spiritual from the physical world stands modern science, with eyes closed and head averted, pronouncing the gulf impassable and bottomless, though she holds in her hand a torch which she need only lower into the depths to show her, her own mistake. But across this chasm, the patient student of Theosophy and Hermetic philosophy has constructed a bridge.

The Platonic Philosopher's Creed

By Thomas Taylor

01. I believe in one first cause of all things, whose nature is so immensely transcendent, that it is even super-essential; and that in consequence of this it cannot properly either be named, or spoken of, or conceived by opinion, or be known, or perceived by any being.

02. I believe, however, that if it be lawful to give a name to that which is truly ineffable, the appellations of *the one* and *the good* are of all others the most adapted to it; the former of these names indicating that it is the principle of all things, and the latter that it is the ultimate object of desire to all things.

03. I believe that this immense principle produced such things as are first and proximate to itself, most similar to itself: just as the heat *immediately* proceeding from fire is most similar to the heat in the fire; and the light *immediately* emanating from the sun, to that which the sun essentially contains. Hence, this principle produces many principles proximately from itself.

04. I likewise believe that since all things differ from each other, and are multiplied with their proper differences, each of these multitudes is suspended from its one proper principle. That, in consequence of this, all beautiful things, whether in souls or in bodies, are suspended from one fountain of beauty. That whatever possesses symmetry, and whatever is true, and all principles are in a certain respect connate with the first principle, so far as they are principles, with an appropriate subjection and analogy. That all other principles are comprehended in this first principle, not with interval and multitude, but as parts in the whole, and number in the monad. That it is not a certain principle like each of the rest; for of

these, one is the principle of beauty, another of truth, and another of something else, but it is *simply principle.* Nor is it simply the *principle of beings,* but it is the *principle of principles;* it being necessary that the characteristic property of principle after the same manner as other things, should not begin from multitude, but should be collected into one monad as a summit, and which is the principle of principles.

05. I believe, therefore, that such things as are produced by the first good in consequence of being connascent with it, do not recede from essential goodness, since they are immoveable and unchanged, and are eternally established in the same blessedness. All other natures, however, being produced, by the one good, and many goodnesses, since they fall off from essential goodness, and are not immovably established in the nature of divine goodness, possess on this account the good according to participation.

06. I believe that as all things considered as subsisting *causally* in this immense principle, are transcendently more excellent than they are when considered as effects proceeding from him; this principle is very properly said to be all things, *prior* to all; priority denoting exempt transcendency. Just as number may be considered as subsisting occultly in the monad, and the circle in the center; this *occult* being the same in each with *causal* subsistence.

07. I believe that the most proper mode of venerating this great principle of principles is to extend in silence the ineffable parturitions of the soul to its ineffable co-sensation; and that if it be at all lawful to celebrate it, it is to be celebrated as a thrice unknown darkness, as the god of all gods, and the unity of all unities, as more ineffable than all silence, and more occult than all essence, as holy among the holies, and concealed in its first progeny, the intelligible gods.

08. I believe that self-subsistent natures are the immediate offspring of this principle, if it be lawful thus to denominate things which ought rather to be called ineffable unfoldings into light from the ineffable.

09. I believe that incorporeal forms or ideas resident in a divine intellect, are the paradigms or models of everything which has a perpetual subsistence according to nature. That these ideas subsist primarily in the highest intellects, secondarily in souls, and ultimately in sensible natures; and that they subsist in each, characterized by the essential properties of the beings in which they are contained. That they possess a *paternal, producing, guardian, connecting, perfective,* and *uniting power.* That in *divine beings* they possess a power fabricative and gnostic; in *nature* a power fabricative but not gnostic; and in *human souls* in their present condition through a degradation of intellect, a power gnostic, but not fabricative.

10. I believe that this world, depending on its divine artificer, who is himself an intelligible world, replete with the archetypal ideas of all things, is perpetually flowing, and perpetually advancing to being, and, compared with its paradigm, has no stability, or reality of being. That considered, however, as animated by a divine soul, and as being the receptacle of divinities from whom bodies are suspended, it is justly called by Plato, a blessed god.

11. I believe that the great body of this world, which subsists in a perpetual dispersion of temporal extension, may be properly called a *whole, with a total subsistence,* or a *whole of wholes,* on account of the perpetuity of its duration, though this is nothing more than a flowing eternity. That the other wholes which it contains are the celestial spheres, the sphere of aether, the whole of air considered as one great orb, the whole earth, and the whole sea. That these spheres are *parts with a total subsistence,* and through this subsistence are perpetual.

12. I believe that all the parts of the universe are unable to participate of the providence of divinity in a similar manner, but some of its parts enjoy this eternally, and others temporarily; some in a primary and others in a secondary degree; for the universe being a perfect whole, must have a first, a middle, and a last part. But its first parts, as having the most excellent subsistence, must always exist according to nature; and its last parts must sometimes exist according to, and sometimes contrary to, nature. Hence, the celestial bodies, which are the first parts of the universe, perpetually subsist according to nature, but the whole spheres, and the multitude co-ordinate to these wholes; and the only alteration which they experience is a mutation of figure, and variation of light at different periods; but in the sublunary region, while the spheres of the elements remain on account of their subsistence, as wholes, always according to nature; the parts of the wholes have sometimes a natural, and sometimes an unnatural subsistence: for thus alone can the circle of generation unfold all the variety which it contains. I believe, therefore, that the different periods in which these mutations happen, are with great propriety called by Plato, periods of *fertility* and sterility: for in these periods a fertility or sterility of men, animals, and plants takes place: so that in fertile periods mankind will be both more numerous, and upon the whole superior in mental and bodily endowments to the men of a barren period. And that a similar reasoning must be extended to irrational animals and plants. I also believe that the most dreadful consequences, attending a barren period with respect to mankind is this, that in such a period they have no scientific theology, and deny the existence of the immediate progeny of the ineffable cause of all things.

13. I believe that as the divinities are eternally good and profitable, but are never noxious, and ever subsist in the same uniform mode of being, that we are conjoined with them

through similitude when we are virtuous, but separated from them through dissimilitude when we are vicious. That while we live according to virtue we partake of the gods, but cause them to be our enemies when we become evil; not that they are angry (for anger is a passion, and they are impassive), but because guilt prevents us from receiving the illuminations of the gods, and subjects us to the power of avenging demons. Hence, I believe, that if we obtain pardon of our guilt through prayers and sacrifices, we neither appease the gods, nor cause any mutation to take place in them; but by methods of this kind, and by our conversion to a divine nature, we apply a remedy to our vices, and again become partakers of the goodness of the gods. So that it is the same thing to assert, that divinity is turned from the evil as to say that the sun is concealed from those who are deprived of sight.

14. I believe that a divine nature is not indigent of anything. But the honors which are paid to the gods, are performed for the sake of the advantage of those who pay them. Hence, since the providence of the gods is extended everywhere, a certain habitude or fitness is all that is requisite for the reception of their beneficent communications. But all habitude is produced through imitation and similitude. On this account temples imitate the heavens, but altars the earth. Statues resemble life, and on this account they are similar to animals. Prayers imitate that which is intellectual; but characters, superior ineffable powers. Herbs and stones resemble matter; and animals which are sacrificed, the irrational life of our souls. From all these, however, I believe that nothing happens to the gods beyond what they already possess; for what accession can be made to a divine nature? But a conjunction of our souls with the gods is by these means effected.

15. I believe that as the world considered as one great comprehending whole is a divine animal, so likewise every whole which it contains is a world, possessing in the first place a self-perfect unity proceeding from the ineffable, by which it becomes a god; in the second place, a divine intellect; in the third place, a divine soul; and in the last place, a deified body. That each of these wholes is the producing cause of all the multitude which it contains, and on this account is said to be a whole prior to parts; because considered as possessing an eternal form which holds all its parts together, and gives to the whole perpetuity of subsistence, it is not indigent of such parts to the perfection of its being. And that it follows by a geometrical necessity that these wholes which rank thus high in the-universe must be animated.

16. Hence I believe that after the immense principle of principles in which all things causally subsist absorbed in super-essential light, and involved in unfathomable depths, a beautiful series of principles proceeds, all largely partaking of the ineffable, all stamped with the occult characters of deity, all possessing an overflowing fullness of good. That from these dazzling summits, these ineffable blossoms, these divine propagations, being, life, intellect soul, nature and body depend; *monads* suspended from *unities,* deified natures proceeding from deities. That each of these monads, is the leader of a series, which extends to the last of things, and which, while it proceeds from, at the same time abides in, and returns to its leader. Thus all beings proceed from and are comprehended in the first being; all intellects emanate from one first intellect; all souls from one first soul; all natures blossom from one first nature; and all bodies proceed from the vital and luminous body of the world. That all these great monads are comprehended in the first one, from which both they and all their depending series are unfolded into light. And that hence this first one is truly the unity of unities, the monad

of monads, the principle of principles, the god of gods, one and all things, and yet one prior to all.

17. I also believe, that of the gods some are mundane, but others supermundane; and that the mundane are those who fabricate the world. But of the supermundane, some produce essences, others intellect, and others soul; and on this account, they are distinguished into three orders. Of the mundane gods also, some are the causes of the existence of the world; others animate it; others again harmonize it, thus composed of different natures; and lastly, others guard and preserve it when harmonically arranged. Since these orders likewise, are four, and each consists of things first, middle, and last, it is necessary that the governors of these should be twelve. Hence Jupiter, Neptune and Vulcan, fabricate the world;. Ceres, Juno, and Diana, animate it; Mercury, Venus, and Apollo, harmonize it; and lastly, Vesta, Minerva and Mars, preside over it with a guardian power. But the truth of this, may be seen in statues, as in enigmas. For Apollo harmonizes the lyre; Pallas is invested with arms; and Venus is naked; since harmony produces beauty, and beauty is not concealed in subjects of sensible inspection. I likewise believe, that as these Gods primarily possess the world, it is necessary to consider the other mundane Gods as subsisting in them; as Bacchus in Jupiter, Asclepius in Apollo, and the Graces in Venus. We may also behold the spheres with which they are connected, *viz.,* Vesta with the earth, Neptune with water, Juno with air, and Vulcan with fire. But Apollo and Diana, are assumed for the sun and moon; the sphere of Saturn is attributed to Ceres; Aether to Pallas; and heaven is common to them all.

18. I also believe that man is a microcosm, comprehending in himself *partially* everything which the world contains divinely and *totally*. That hence he is endued with an intellect subsisting in energy, and a rational soul proceeding

from the same causes as those from which the intellect and soul of the universe proceed. And that he has likewise an ethereal vehicle analogous to the heavens, and a terrestrial body composed from the four elements, and with which also it is co-ordinate.

19. I believe that the rational part of man, in which his essence consists is of a self-motive nature, and that it subsists between intellect, which is immoveable both in essence and energy, and nature, which both moves and is moved.

20. I believe that the human as well as every mundane soul, uses periods and restitutions of its proper life. For in consequence of being measured by time, it energizes transitively, and possesses a proper motion. But everything which is moved perpetually, and participates of time, revolves periodically, and proceeds from the same to the same.

21. I also believe that as the human soul ranks among the number of those souls that *sometimes* follow the mundane divinities, in consequence of subsisting immediately after daemons and heroes the *perpetual* attendants of the gods, it possesses a power of descending infinitely into the sublunary region, and of ascending from thence to real being. That in consequence of this, the soul while an inhabitant of earth is in a fallen condition, an apostate from deity, an exile from the orb of light. That she can only be restored while on earth to the divine likeness, and be able after death to re-ascend to the intelligible world, by the exercise of the *cathartic* and *theoretic* virtues; the former purifying her from the defilements of a mortal nature, and the latter elevating her to the vision of true being. And that such a soul returns after death to her kindred star from which she fell, and enjoys a blessed life.

22. I believe that the human soul essentially contains all knowledge, and that whatever knowledge she acquires in the

present life, is nothing more than a recovery of what she once possessed; and which discipline evocates from its dormant retreats.

23. I also believe that the soul is punished in a future for the crimes she has committed in the present life; but that this punishment is proportioned to the crimes, and is not perpetual; divinity punishing, not from anger or revenge, but in order to purify the guilty soul, and restore her to the proper perfection of her nature.

24. I also believe that the human soul on its departure from the present life, will, if not properly purified, pass into other terrene bodies; and that if it passes into a human body, it becomes the soul of that body; but if into the body of a brute, it does not become the soul of the brute, but is externally connected with the brutal soul in the same manner as presiding daemons are connected in their beneficent operations with mankind; for the rational part never becomes the soul of the irrational nature.

25. Lastly, I believe that souls that live according to virtue, shall in other respects be happy; and when separated from the irrational nature, and purified from all body, shall be conjoined with the gods, and govern the whole world, together with the deities by whom it was produced.

Plato's Conception of the Function of True Art

By Fritz Sage Darrow

According to Plato, each man is born furnished with innate ideas - the inheritance garnered by the Soul during former existences. The object of education, then, is to uncover these ideas, or in the words of Katherine Tingley, the Leader and Official Head of the Universal Brotherhood and Theosophical Society:

> The real secret of true education is rather to evolve the child's character than to overtax the child's mind: it is to bring out, rather than to bring to the faculties of the child. The grander part is from within. . . . It means no less than the development of the Soul, with all the capabilities which belong to it. . . . It is the power to live in harmony with our environment, the power to draw out from the recesses of our own nature all the potentialities of character and divine life. . . . *It is not so much a something which is imparted. It is a liberation from the powers of the lower forces which hinder and check a growth which ought to be unchecked and spontaneous.*

This characteristically Theosophical attitude of Plato toward life and education makes it imperative, in interpreting the philosopher's statements, to *read between the lines.* Consequently, his conception of the function of true art has been sadly misunderstood even by excellent scholars, for not a few have gone so far as to declare that he showed himself entirely unacquainted with the essence of art by accusing the arts of being imitative.

The truth, however, is that Plato did not criticize the arts from any misunderstanding, but, strange as the paradox may at first seem, because of the very keenness and intensity of his appreciation of the artistic ideal. To realize Plato's position, his declarations regarding art in the *Phaedrus*, the *Philebus*, and the *Symposium*, are fully as important - if not more important - than the criticisms contained in the *Republic*. In the *Republic* he criticizes the degenerate arts of his own day, but in the *Phaedrus*, the *Philebus*, and the *Symposium*, he reveals glimpses of his conception of the ideal or heavenly art.

In Plato there are two men, the man of imagery, the poet; and the man of fact, the moralist. Temperamentally he was endowed with the keenest appreciation of art, and his real doctrine as to the function of true art, that of harmony within and without, is both moral and aesthetic. His criticism of the arts, as ordinarily practiced, arises from no indifference to beauty but in very fact from his great love of beauty. His idealism goes hand in hand with his criticism.

Although Plato's idea of the Good was influential in determining the character of his criticism of the arts, he did not confuse ethics with aesthetics, for in the *Republic* he says:

> The man is a fool, who laughs or directs the shafts of his ridicule at any other sight than that of folly and vice, or seriously inclines to measure the Beautiful by any other standard than that of the Good. (Book V, 452, e)

The same thought has been nobly expressed by Katherine Tingley:

> Only that art is true art that leads the student daily nearer the golden portals of the Life Beautiful.

An important factor in Platonic philosophy is the recognition that human nature is essentially imitative, naturally assimilating itself to its surroundings.

Did you never observe how imitations beginning in early youth, at last sink into the constitution and become a second nature of body, voice, and mind? (*Republic*, Book III, d)

Man is like a plant which having proper nurture, grows and matures into all virtue, but if sown and planted in an alien soil, becomes the most noxious of all weeds, unless saved by some divine help. (*Republic*, Book VI, 492, a)

Let our artists rather be those who are gifted to discern the true nature of beauty and grace; then will our youth dwell in a land of health, amid fair sights and sounds; and beauty, the effluence of fair works, will meet the sense like a breeze, and insensibly draw the Soul even in childhood into harmony with the beauty of reason. (*Republic*, Book III, 401, c-d)

To the ancient Greeks, and to Plato preeminently, rhythm and harmony, law and order, were closely allied to reason. Thus the outer world, when rightly interpreted, speaks in the same language as the inner; and the inanimate, so-called, holds communion with the animate. Environment has a suggestive influence upon the Soul. Hence the importance of art and the necessity for an ethical censorship over all the arts from painting to poetry. The arts, rightly regulated, must express something worth expressing, and poetry and music, ordinarily regarded merely as accomplishments, become integral parts of education. This is one of the great lessons of Hellenism, which Theosophy is re-incorporating into the life of today, for Katherine Tingley has said:

Music is usually regarded as an amusement, a relaxation, and nothing more. At Point Loma it becomes a part of life itself, and one of those subtle forces of nature which, rightly applied, calls into activity the divine powers of the soul.

There is held to be an immense correspondence between music on the one hand and thought and aspiration upon the other, and only that deserves the name of music to which the noblest and the purest aspirations are responsive. Music is a part of the daily life at the Point (Point Loma), not merely as an exercise which occupies its stated time and seasons, but as a principle which animates all the activities.

There is a science of consciousness, and into that science music can enter more largely than is usually supposed.

The Theosophist, therefore, agrees with Plato who conceives of art "not as a collection of canons of criticism, but rather as a subtle influence, which pervades all things."

Is not this, I said, the reason, Glancon, why musical training is so powerful: because rhythm and harmony find their way into the secret places of the soul, on which they mightily fasten, bearing grace in their movements, and making the soul graceful of him who is rightly educated and ungraceful if ill-educated; and also because he who has received *the true education of the inner being* will most keenly perceive omissions or faults in art and nature, and with a true taste, while he praises and rejoices over, and receives into his soul the good, he will justly blame and hate the bad, now in the clays of his youth, even before he is able to know the reason of the thing; and when reason comes he will recognize and salute her as a friend with whom his education has made him long familiar? (*Republic*, III, d; 402, a)

Therefore Plato, the Theosophist, maintained that all true education has for its object the improvement of the soul, and conceived of it as consisting of all the spiritual influences by which the Higher nature is nourished and quick-ened. (L. R. Nettleship: *Plato's Conception of the Good*, page 383)

It should be noted that this conception of Plato is in entire agreement with art as practiced at Point Loma, where in the words of Katherine Tingley:

> It follows faithfully upon the lines of the Science of the Soul which it is our mission to revive. Under this Science it becomes the true expression of the Soul ideals, and both art and decoration are no longer adventitious or capricious additions to our environment, but they become integral parts of that to which they belong.

Whatever has in any way a right to exist must contain within itself the possibility of existing beautifully. The power of beautiful expression is not an affair of custom, nor convention, nor from books. It comes from the arousing of the inner powers of the Soul which are in sympathy with whatever is high and pure.

L. R. Nettleship has pointed out that Two feelings struggle in Plato: the feeling of what art may do for men, and the feeling of the evil that is often associated with it; and the result of this conflict is the idea that art can only be made serviceable in the world by limiting it. (*Lectures on the Republic of Plato*, page 169)

In this limitation it is the artistic Greek who is dictating - the man in whom the principle of proportion and moderation is predominant - the man swayed by the sentiment of "nothing too much." The idea of limit, of defining principle, pervades all Greek thought, and is a strong motive influencing Plato in his criticism of the arts, which he sought to purify by the aid of the ideal art which instinctively discerns " the true nature of beauty and grace." Therefore the arts are of superlative importance in Plato's eyes because of the imitative character of human nature and because of their inherent power.

By nature Plato was an artist, by reflection a moralist. Therefore in his criticism we have an artist criticizing the arts and his judgment is that of an Initiate. Since the philosopher possesses the wonderful and rare power of a double imagination, an imagination which is both sensuous and metaphysical, the proverb is right: "if Zeus should descend to the earth he would speak in the style of Plato."

The wise man will always be desirous of preserving the harmony of the body for the sake of the concord of the Soul. (*Republic*, IX, 591, d)

A conclusive proof that Plato is no harsh and unsympathetic critic of the arts, no narrow-minded Puritan, is given by his Hellenicism, his liberal- mindedness, for Hellenicism is the consideration of the essential interests of man, the distinguishing between accretions and organic members, a lesson in rationality. Says Emerson: " Perpetual modernness is the measure of merit in every work of art," and this quality is pre-eminently Plato's, whose "broad humanity transcends all sectional lines."

Plato arraigns the arts, as ordinarily practiced, on two bases: first, philosophically, because they are imitative; and secondly, practically, because they over-stimulate the emotional element of the Soul at the expense and to the detriment of the rational element. He declares that the proper end of art is ethical, and that the artist stands in the position of a teacher. Therefore he condemns in no uncertain tones the deteriorated forms of the arts on the ground that they are governed by no rational principle. Consequently they must be limited and must act as handmaidens to philosophy, the love of wisdom, for the function of the Soul is to synthesize life and to exercise rationality.

"Since the interest of each of the arts is the perfection of each of them, (*Republic*, I, 341, d) - a profound thought of great beauty - the science of life, which stands supreme over all the arts, must be in itself the art of life, and the function of the true artist is to express the beauty of the world as a rhythm and a harmony expressing rationality. Platonic ethics are inseparably linked with Platonic aesthetics. The true art of life is to live well, and not, as some have supposed, to do away with all art. The ultimate is not only the Good but it is also the True and the Beautiful. Plato's aim is to establish the heavenly beauty on earth.

Therefore he criticizes the existent arts because of their lack of principle and their aimless variation, their miscellaneous empiricism and their failure to conform to a standard of truth and nobility. He applies four criteria in purging the arts, namely, the standards of consistency, truth, proportion, and simplicity. Art which merely panders to pleasure and which is not under ethical jurisdiction is a specious flattery, a false rhetoric.

The only true art in Plato's ideal is the art of living, which, when practiced, will produce the all-beautiful. He protests against the arts as disconnected features in experience, and declares that they must be organized, synthesized.

The function of true art is to convey a knowledge of the truth. (*Phaedrus*, 262)

The outcome of this censorship of the arts is to make mind the king of both heaven and earth. (*Philebus*, 28, c)

Knowledge is one; yet the various parts of knowledge have each of them a particular name, and consequently there are many arts and sciences. (*Sophist*, 257)

If we are not able to hunt the good with one idea only, with three we may take our prey: beauty, symmetry, truth are the three. (*Philebus*, 65, a)

The mind of the philosopher alone has wings. (*Phaedrus*, 249, c)

He is a lover of the sight of truth, (*Republic.* V, 475, e) and unlike the mere sight-seer or curiosity-seeker has a vision of absolute beauty. (*Republic*, V, 476)

Therefore he alone, who is able to perceive the eternal world where ideas dwell, is the true artist, and art should be subordinate to philosophy or the love of wisdom.

Beauty is certainly a soft, smooth, slippery thing and therefore of a nature which easily steps in and permeates our souls. And I further add that the Good is the Beautiful. (*Lysis*, 216)

At length, the vision is revealed-of a single science, which is the science of beauty everywhere. (*Symposium*, 210, d)

www.ingramcontent.com/pod-product-compliance
Lightning Source LLC
LaVergne TN
LVHW041500070426
835507LV00009B/720